Designed by Flowerpot Press
www.FlowerpotPress.com
CHC-0909-0591
ISBN: 978-1-4867-2564-9
Made in China/Fabriqué en Chine

HOW DO BIRDS SING A DUET?

A BOOK ABOUT BIRD BEHAVIOR

written by clayton tobias grider

illustrated by srimalie bassani

Birds are interesting and wonderful creatures. If you go outside, you most likely will see a bird—they pop up all over the place! In a big city, there are large, plump pigeons waddling around the streets. In rural areas, you may see robins and cardinals or even a huge hawk in the sky! The biggest bird in the world, the ostrich, can be up to 9 feet (2.7 meters) tall! The smallest bird in the world, the bee hummingbird, is only on average 2.3 inches (5.8 centimeters) long.

There are about ten thousand species of birds in the world. Most know how to fly, but there are birds that prefer to stay on the ground. For example, penguins cannot fly, but are very good at swimming. There is so much to learn about birds, so let's begin!

FUN FACT
A bird is considered a bird if it has feathers, a beak, and it lays hard-shelled eggs.

Woah, you're tall!

How do some birds know when to fly south for the winter?
Do they keep a calendar in their nests so they can keep track of the date?

No, but they do have a kind of clock inside their brain that tells them when it is time to move. This internal "clock" responds to things like sunlight and can tell migratory birds, or birds that seasonally fly together in a group to a new location, when it's time to fly south. During winter in the Northern Hemisphere, the days get shorter and that signals to the migratory birds that it is time to go.

Once the birds know when to go south, how do they know how to get there? Scientists are still learning different ways that some of our feathered friends make their way south. Some researchers believe that a bird can "smell" their way across the flight path that they follow every year. Some birds, like Canada geese, are believed to use past experiences and landmarks to tell them where to go.

Canada goose

FUN FACT

Migrating Canada geese return to the exact same nesting locations every year.

Migratory birds have increased fat reserves to fuel migration.

The northern wheatear will cover 9,000 miles (14,484 kilometers) each way on its migration—impressive for a bird that weighs less than one ounce (28.3 grams)!

Migration is very important to birds. Of the over 2,000 species of birds in North America, over 350 of them migrate. The process of moving to warmer climates is a vital part of a cycle that allows these birds to survive. The northern wheatear travels from Alaska across Siberia and central Asia to its wintering grounds in eastern Africa. You would have to hop on an airplane and fly from New York City to Los Angeles and back TWICE to travel as far as the northern wheatear flies each year.

northern wheatear

HAIRY WOODPECKER

A worm! Yummy!

How does a woodpecker know where to peck to find their food? Do they set up a camera near a tree to see what's inside?

No, woodpeckers don't use cameras, they use their beaks!

Woodpeckers are so cool!

RED-HEADED WOODPECKER

PILEATED WOODPECKER

As woodpeckers scale a tree trunk, they tap lightly on the bark. Wood-boring insects leave hollow tunnels in the trees they invade and the tapping from a woodpecker's beak makes a noise that alerts the bird to the insects hiding inside. They can also sometimes smell and hear the insects feeding on the wood inside. Some ants and beetles leave an especially strong smell, allowing the woodpeckers to find exactly where they may be hiding.

tongue

Once a woodpecker locates a bug, it will drill a hole into the tree trunk with its beak. Then it will use its very long tongue to reach into the tree to grab the bug. That's right—a woodpecker's tongue is super long! It is so long that in order to store it, their tongue has to curl around the back of the bird's skull. Most woodpecker species also have barbs or sticky saliva on their tongue that can help them grab the bugs they find inside trees.

Amazing!

FUN FACT
There are many different kinds of woodpeckers and not all of them choose to eat insects. Some enjoy berries, nuts, seeds, and even sap. (Shout-out to the yellow-bellied sapsucker!)

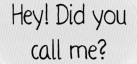
Hey! Did you call me?

Searching for food is not the only reason for a woodpecker to peck. Woodpeckers also communicate with one another by hammering loudly and rapidly on tree trunks.
This process is known as drumming.
Since woodpeckers do not chirp and sing like some other birds, researchers think that drumming signals to other woodpeckers where their territory is and helps them communicate with potential mates.

How does a pelican fly without flapping its wings? Does it use a hot-air balloon to help take it where it needs to go?

No, but pelicans do take advantage of wind to fly without flapping their wings in a process called gliding.

Now I can just sit back and relax!

As a pelican's wings move through the air, they are held at a slight angle, which deflects the air around them gently downward. This creates an opposite force that pushes the bird upwards. You can feel this force if you carefully tilt your hand outside the window of a moving car when there is a strong wind. You will feel your hand lifting up from the wind! This opposite force is called lift.

lift

velocity

drag

weight

Even with the help of lift, a pelican cannot stay in the air forever. There are things that slow them down and they must dive toward the earth in order to maintain a gliding speed. Eventually, the pelican either has to land or flap its wings, but gliding allows the pelican to get to a location without using too much energy.

lift

wind

There is another way that other gliding birds can stay in the air longer. Some birds, like condors, take advantage of air currents. Warm air rises, so if a bird can find one of these warm air currents, called a thermal, it can use it to rise higher and higher into the sky. When the bird gets high enough, it leaves the thermal and can continue soaring in the sky for a while without flapping its wings. By taking advantage of the thermals, the birds do not need to use as much energy and can take breaks while making long treks.

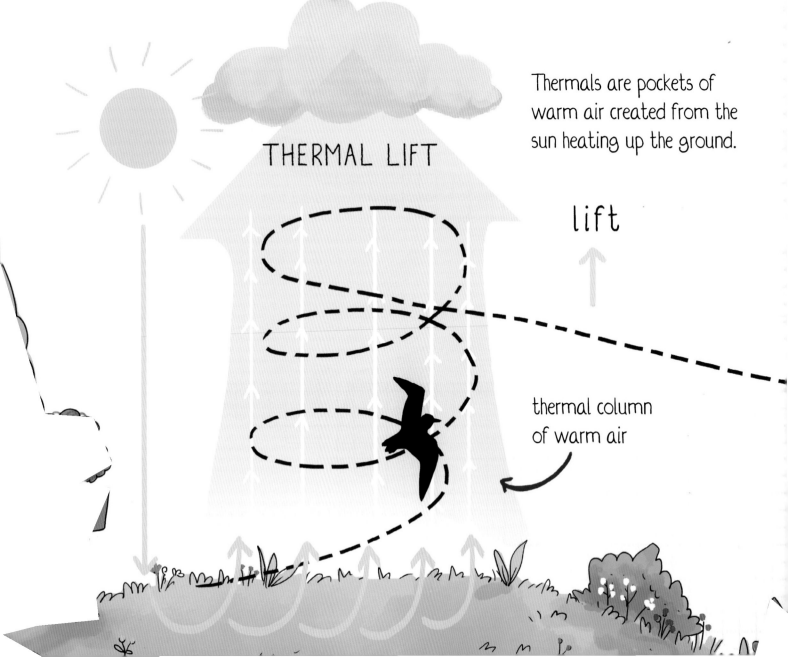

THERMAL LIFT

Thermals are pockets of warm air created from the sun heating up the ground.

lift

thermal column of warm air

There is another type of strategic soaring called dynamic soaring. Birds that use this technique use different wind speeds at different heights in the sky to their advantage. By diving in and out of faster winds, birds can maintain flight for a longer time. Albatrosses use this technique to support their multi-year voyages across the seas and around the world.

COOLER AIR DESCENDS

sink

Energy saving soar activated!

Why do Canada geese fly in V formations? Is it because V is their favorite letter in the alphabet?

No, it's not their favorite letter! Well, it might be, who knows. They actually fly like this for two main reasons: to conserve energy and to keep track of everyone.

The vortex produced by the front bird's wings pushes the air up so the geese behind it can lift up and fly a little easier.

FUN FACT
A collection of flying geese is called a skein!

I'm a little tired up here. Who wants to take a turn being the leader?

I'll take the lead!

When Canada geese fly in this formation, each bird flies slightly above the bird in front of them. Because they do this, the wind does not get in the way of the birds in the back, which makes flying easier. When the bird in the front of the V gets tired, they just move to the back of the V. That way, every bird in the skein takes a turn at the front and helps the other geese out.

Researchers have discovered that when families of geese migrate together, the parents take turns at the front of the V. The younger geese take up the rear, where they do not need to be as strong as their parents.

The other reason Canada geese fly in a V formation is to keep track of everyone, especially at night. The V shape allows the geese to easily see the other geese they are with so they can all keep an eye on each other and know exactly which direction to go.

Is it time for a break yet? I'm hungry!

Geese migrate in stages. They stop at places along the way to rest and eat food. The stop is not always the same every single year. They can change it for a number of reasons, for example if the availability of food changes in a specific area. Geese from the northernmost areas of North America travel the farthest south. Southern populations of geese do not migrate as far. This is called leapfrog migration, and scientists are still trying to learn why they do this. Although some scientists have suggested that it is so they do not compete for food with the southern populations of geese.

No, but they do sing to get attention! Researchers show that songbirds sing in order to defend their territories and to impress potential mates.

Birds make a lot of noises and each one is distinct and serves a different purpose. For example, a bird song is different from a bird call. A bird call tends to be shorter and less rhythmic.

Look out everyone!

Birds produce sounds using a syrinx, which is an organ located in the bird's throat. The syrinx allows a bird to produce two unrelated pitches at once. Some birds can create rising and falling notes at the same time!

If you hear a beautiful bird song, you are most likely hearing a male bird. Most female songbirds in temperate climates use short calls, while the males produce longer and more complex songs. In tropical climates, females are more likely to sing. Many tropical songbirds sing together in what is called duetting—kind of like they are in a band!

Some birds are born with the knowledge to sing their songs, but most songbirds have to learn how to sing. They begin learning their songs while in the nest. This is known as the critical period. The young birds listen to the adult birds sing around them. When they get old enough, young birds attempt to copy their parents and practice until they are just like them—kind of like how you learn to talk. Some birds, like mockingbirds, even learn to mimic other birds' songs and even other species, such as frogs and cats!

How do birds build their homes? Do they hire professionals to come and build them a luxury home?

No, they don't need to hire anyone. Most birds take on the task of building their nests and shelters themselves. Each bird species uses its own techniques to craft a unique place to live. Chaffinches nest in trees and use sticky spiderwebs to make pads on the branches which anchors their nest to the tree.

Waterbirds and seabirds

These birds all nest on the ground near water. Waterbirds prefer freshwater lakes and streams, while seabirds occupy (but are not restricted to) salty or brackish coastal wetlands.

lichens

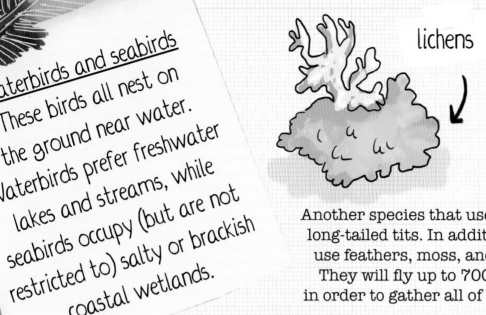

feathers

Another species that uses spiderwebs are the long-tailed tits. In addition to spiderwebs, they use feathers, moss, and lichens to create their home. They will fly up to 700 miles (1,126.5 kilometers) in order to gather all of the materials they need.

Some birds do not work as hard to find a nest; they use holes that already exist. Owls, for example, use holes in trees as a ready-made place to raise their young.

Owl nest inside a hole in a tree

Mallard duck near a lake

dog fur

Sparrow nest
in a gutter

Sparrow nest
in a gutter

House sparrows and starlings use holes in roofs to make their nests. All they need to do is line the hole with grass or moss in order to call your home their home!

Birds will use any available material that they can carry to build their nests. Leaves, sticks, mosses, lichens, feathers, and even animal fur are all materials that birds utilize. In some species, a male bird's skill at nest building is a sign of his suitability as a mate. Male Eurasian wrens build multiple nests to attract females. While cardinals like to share the work and both the male and female help to build the nests (although females tend to do most of the building).

Cardinal family

female

male

leaves
and sticks

OFFICIAL NATIONAL BIRDS

Do you know that many countries around the globe have an official national bird? Learn about some of the national birds from around the world. How many do you recognize?

BALD EAGLE National Bird of the United States

Bald eagles are considered an American symbol and are featured on the quarter and the Great Seal of the United States. They are large birds that can dive fast to catch their prey.

Location: Every US state (besides Hawaii), Canada, and northern Mexico

Habitat: Often found near water, such as rivers and lakes, where they catch fish to eat, or high in trees, where they nest.

Diet: Carnivore

Length: ~2.8 feet (0.9 meters)

Weight: ~9 pounds (4.1 kilograms)

Wingspan: ~6.7 feet (2 meters)

Differences between males and females: Female bald eagles are larger than males.

Fun fact: Bald eagles can fly up to 10,000 feet (3,048 meters) in the sky.

ANDEAN CONDOR
National Bird of Chile

GOLDEN EAGLE
National Bird of Mexico

CLAY-COLORED THRUSH
National Bird of Costa Rica

INDIAN PEAFOWL National Bird of India

Indian peafowls are well known for the intense colors and patterns that peacocks display on their tail feathers, known as a train. Peafowls travel in small groups and, despite their large size, are capable of flight, which they use to escape dangerous situations.

Location: Throughout the Indian subcontinent

Habitat: Mainly seen on the ground in open forest areas, where they can be found foraging for berries and grains or eating snakes and lizards.

Diet: Omnivore

Length: ~3.3 feet (1 meter)

Weight: ~9.7 pounds (4.4 kilograms)

Wingspan: ~4.7 feet (1.4 meters)

Differences between males and females: Male peafowls are called peacocks and have blue feathers on their face and bodies and brightly colored tail feathers that fan out. Females are called peahens and have white faces with brownish feathers on the rest of their body. Peahens are also smaller than peacocks.

Fun fact: Peacocks are not born with their trains. Instead, it usually takes them about three years to grow them.

COMMON NIGHTINGALE
National Bird of Iran

GREEN PHEASANT
National Bird of Japan

SRI LANKAN JUNGLEFOWL
National Bird of Sri Lanka

KIWI National Bird of New Zealand

Kiwis are small nocturnal birds with long legs and long beaks. Their long legs allow them to run very fast. In fact, they can easily outrun a human. This comes in handy, as they are flightless birds. Even though they cannot fly, much like their distant cousins the emu and ostrich, they do have small wings.

Location: New Zealand

Habitat: Found at night only in forests or swampy grasslands where they mainly feed on worms, small insects, and plants.

Diet: Omnivore

Length: ~16 inches (40.6 centimeters)

Weight: ~4.2 pounds (1.9 kilograms)

Wingspan: ~1 inch (2.5 centimeters)

Differences between males and females: Female kiwis are heavier and larger than males. They also lay and protect their eggs.

Fun fact: Unlike other birds, kiwi chicks are born with feathers.

COMMON KESTREL
National Bird of Belgium

GYRFALCON
National Bird of Iceland

WHITE STORK
National Bird of Lithuania

BLACK CROWNED CRANE

National Bird of Nigeria

Black crowned cranes are named for their black coloring in addition to the gold feathers on their head that resemble a crown. Black crowned cranes make honking noises, similar to a goose.

Location: Countries throughout northern Africa ranging from Senegal to Ethiopia

Habitat: Found in marshes, grasslands, wetlands, and meadows.

Diet: Omnivore

Length: ~3.3 feet (1 meter)

Weight: ~8 pounds (3.6 kilograms)

Wingspan: ~6.3 feet (1.9 meters)

Differences between adults and juveniles:
Young black crowned cranes have mostly gray feathers and a brown crown in comparison to the black feathers and gold crown of adults.

Fun fact: Black crowned cranes can live for up to 25 years!

RUFOUS HORNERO
National Bird of Argentina

SCARLET MACAW
National Bird of Honduras

GREY CROWNED CRANE
National Bird of Uganda

MAKE YOUR OWN BIRD FEEDER

Want to learn more about birds? Attract them to your yard so you can see them up close with this easy to make bird feeder!

WHAT YOU WILL NEED:

- String (about 18 inches (45 centimeters) long)
- Pine cone
- Peanut butter (shortening can be substituted if you have a nut allergy)
- Birdseed

STEP 1: Take your pine cone and tie the string around the top. Make sure you leave room on the string to be able to tie the remaining length of string to a tree or branch.

STEP 2: Spread peanut butter over the pine cone making sure the outside is completely coated.

STEP 3: Roll the pine cone in birdseed until it is fully covered. Smaller seeds will stick better than bigger ones, but if there are any gaps in the pine cone, you can plug them up with sunflower seeds or other larger seeds.

STEP 4: Hang your feeder up and wait for the birds to come eat!

TIP: Make sure you hang your feeder somewhere where the squirrels won't be able to get to it! A great place to hang your feeder is a high, thin branch.